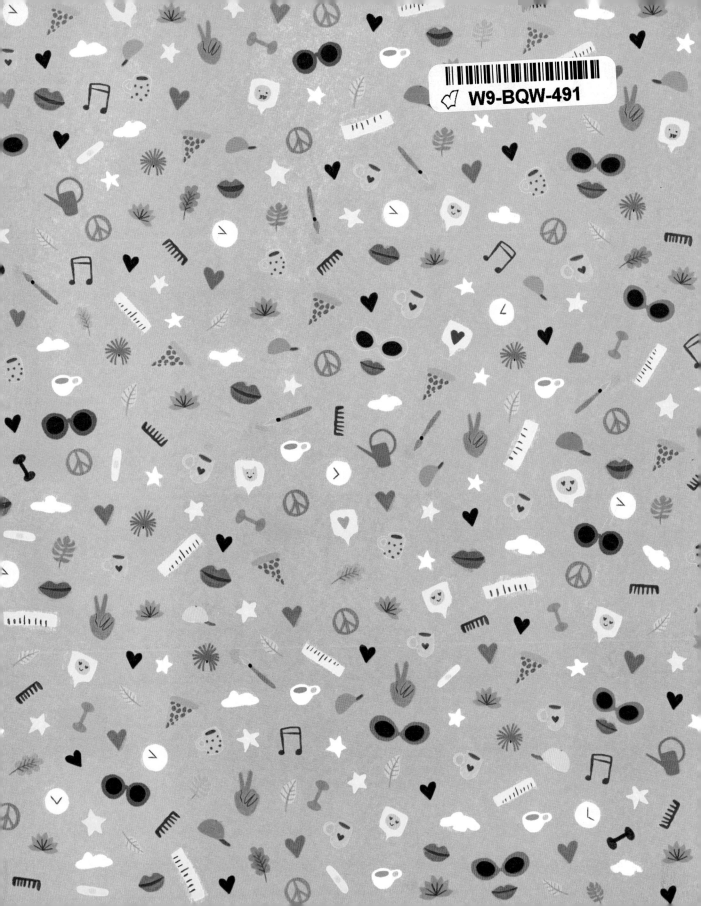

How to spot a mom

WIDE EYED EDITIONS

Moms are talented creatures.

They can be breakfast chefs in the morning, and transform into a human calculator to help with your math homework by the time you get home from school.

Every mom is unique and special in their own way, although many have a similar set of skills.

In this book, you'll learn about lots of different types of mom and how to spot them. There's likely to be some you know already, and you might discover a few you haven't yet met.

Let's celebrate
every one of them!

What is a mom?

A mom is someone's guardian.
That might sound quite simple, but becoming
a mom can happen in lots of ways.

Everyone has a biological mom,
but some also have an adopted mom,
foster moms, or step moms.

They might take care of just one child,
or it could be quite a few.

Some do it all by themselves,
and sometimes children get two moms.

Every type of mom has the same job:
to keep their children safe,
and to guide them through their life.

Anatomy of a mom

EYES
Always on the lookout to keep her family safe.

EARS
Open and ready to listen to giggles, stories, and questions.

MOUTH
Used regularly for directions, vital instructions, and dispensing kisses.

FUNNY BONE
Can be quite large in some.

MIND
Packed with ready-to-be-shared anecdotes and wisdom.

NOSE
Excellent for sniffing out mischief.

HEART
Bottomless and fierce.

GUT
A useful organ for making decisions.

MUSCLES
Honed to carry the heaviest of shopping bags, school backpacks, and cumbersome strollers.

Special mom skills

Being a mom is a big, demanding job. There aren't many breaks, and moms have to be available every day of the week. They're expected to be patient, selfless, strong, and kind—and that's usually without very much sleep!

There are some things that moms can do better than anyone else.
Do you recognize any of these super-mom skills?

Treating scrapes and soothing ills

Solving mysteries and detecting fibs

Listening, nodding, and offering advice

Solving problems with a simple solution

Calming down scary situations

Magically creating the perfect Halloween costume

Managing lots of things at exactly the same time

Moms around the world

There are around two billion moms in the world—you really can't avoid them! The way they bring up their children is often influenced by where they live. Can you think of any traditions your mom might have picked up from where you were born?

US
Mom

Mother's Day has been a national holiday in the US since 1914. It was founded by an American woman called Anna Jarvis, who wanted to celebrate her own mother.

THE NETHERLANDS
Mamma

"Beschuit met Muisjes" (mice biscuits) are biscuits with sugared seeds on top which are served by Dutch moms on the arrival of a new baby.

BRAZIL
Mãe

Birthdays are a big deal in Brazil, especially the first. Moms will often arrange a big party for friends, family, and neighbors with a tiered cake.

NIGER
Maman / Mama

Women in Niger have the most children in the world. On average, almost eight each!

FINLAND
Äiti

When Finnish moms give birth, they are given a box with baby essentials from the government including bedding, diapers, and lots of things to keep them warm. The babies can even sleep inside the box!

CHINA
Māmā

The Azalea flower is the perfect choice for moms in China, as it represents love and womanhood.

VIETNAM
Mẹ

Many Vietnamese moms carry their babies on their backs using a special carrier called a "Hmong carrier."

INDIA
Maan

After having a baby, new Indian moms often go back to live with their moms to help them adapt to parenthood.

The outdoorsy mom

This mom always looks a little windswept. A bit of rain doesn't put her off, and creepy crawlies don't scare her. She's got a nose for adventure and never misses a chance to bring the family out with her, whether it's a mountain hike or a "short" bike ride. There might be a few grumbles on the way, but she knows they'll love it once they're out there!

NATURAL HABITAT: *Around a campfire*

LIKES: *Fresh air, brisk walks, nature*

DISLIKES: *Concrete*

HOW TO SPOT: *She's got all the gear, and all the get up and go!*

NATURAL HABITAT: *Indoors, preferably on the couch*
LIKES: *Take-out treats and pyjama parties*
DISLIKES: *Being too cold, being too warm, and worst of all—getting wet*
HOW TO SPOT: *Usually found underneath a blanket*

The homebody

This stay-in mom loves family adventures, too—she just prefers using cushions and quilts to build her tents, and the only wildlife she likes to watch is on-screen! Her home is a cozy haven, perfect for snuggling on the couch with her family. She's at her best in her slippers and pyjamas, a cup of hot cocoa in one hand and the TV controller in the other.

The coach

This competitive mom always gives 110%. She knows her kids have what it takes to get to number one and she never leaves anything to chance. Some might call her pushy, but she's too busy winning to let them bother her! And her competitive nature doesn't end with her kids. She takes the charity fun run VERY seriously, too. A loss isn't the end of the world in her family—there's always a next time.

NATURAL HABITAT: On the side lines (pacing)

LIKES: Giving motivating pep talks and high fives

DISLIKES: Losing

HOW TO SPOT: Usually side-eyeing the competition

The cheerleader

"Give me a Y! Give me an A! Give me a Y! What does it spell? ... YAY!"
This proud parent believes there's no such thing as too much encouragement.
She's her child's biggest fan and is always there to cheer them on. Nearly every
inch of her home is decorated with report cards and "interesting" art projects
pinned to the walls. Winning doesn't really matter to this enthusiastic mom—
she's just happy for a chance to hold a banner with her child's name on it.

NATURAL HABITAT: *The front row*
LIKES: *Rooting for the underdog*
DISLIKES: *Negativity*
HOW TO SPOT: *Often sports T-shirts with inspirational quotes*

The chatty mom

We all know a chatty mom. No matter where she goes, from the school to the supermarket, the drugstore to the swimming pool, there will always be somebody she knows. Her family have learned that "I'll just say hello" is really code for "I'll be back in an hour." On the plus side, dinner time in this mom's house is always a lively event—she's full of questions about her children's day, and always has a funny story to share.

NATURAL HABITAT: *In front of a line of people*

LIKES: *An audience*

DISLIKES: *Libraries*

HOW TO SPOT: *Usually accompanied by a bored child attempting to get her back on track!*

TIPS FOR CHILDREN OF CHATTY MOMS

1. Create a diversion

2. Offer her some candy

3. Laugh at strange parts of her conversation so that she has to take you aside to check if you're OK

4. Tell her you've organized a sponsored silence

5. Give up and ask for some earmuffs

The trendy mom

This fashion-forward mom is always on trend. Her kids' closets are perfectly organized by color AND item, and she's always up to date with the coolest looks and brands. She has a magic way of zhuzhing hair so that even the most complicated hair styles are a breeze, making her children the envy of the playground. No matter what she does, she does it with style. She can even make a rainy weekend at a campsite look chic, thanks to the matching raincoats her family is decked out in.

NATURAL HABITAT: Her closet
LIKES: Planning the perfect look
DISLIKES: Bad hair days
HOW TO SPOT: She can make the supermarket aisle look like a runway

NATURAL HABITAT: *The garage*

LIKES: *DIY*

DISLIKES: *Throwing anything away*

HOW TO SPOT: *Usually up a ladder or wielding a power tool*

The practical mom

"Always be prepared" is this mom's mantra. When it comes to choosing clothes, the first question in her mind is often: "does it have pockets?" You'll rarely see her without a trusty (and seemingly bottomless) handbag, which is always full of essentials such as bandages, wet wipes, pins, and snacks. From fixing broken toys to wiping runny noses—nothing phases her.

The online mom

There's not much that this mom doesn't know about the digital world. Her kids never have to explain an internet trend—she's already in the loop. Her skills don't end there—she's also a pro at video calling the extended family, online shopping, and group chats. The internet is her go-to source for answers to all her parenting questions, and her phone is always by her side, ready for the next status update.

NATURAL HABITAT: *Anywhere with WIFI*

LIKES: *Emojis*

DISLIKES: *A slow connection*

HOW TO SPOT: *Often commenting a little too much on her kids' social media posts*

AN ONLINE MOM'S SEARCH HISTORY

"How to teach grandparents to video call"

"Babies eating lemons for the first time"

"How to remove spit-up stains"

"Otters holding hands asleep"

"Is my child a genius?"

"How much sleep can humans survive on?"

The boss mom

Boss mom is always in charge. Only those who are feeling extra brave question her instructions. She may seem a little strict, but she only wants what's best for her family. She's a big believer in consequences—if you want to learn the saxophone, she'll let you on one condition: no quitting!

NATURAL HABITAT: The head of the table
LIKES: Tough love
DISLIKES: Rebellion
HOW TO SPOT: She's always the leader—from the family meeting to the conga line!

The zen mom

For this laid-back mom, everything that will be, will be. She believes there isn't much that can't be worked out after a long handstand and a cup of herbal tea. This mom sees herself as a guide for her children rather than a leader and loves to watch them make their own choices. She likes to keep her loved ones close, with a carrier for the small ones and a warm embrace for the larger ones.

NATURAL HABITAT: *Sitting on a mat, quietly meditating*

LIKES: *Eco-friendly tote bags and natural remedies*

DISLIKES: *Busy supermarkets*

HOW TO SPOT: *In her house, shoes are optional!*

The sporty mom

This leggings-lover is bursting with energy and always up for a challenge. She loves to bring family and exercise together. You'll find her jogging in the park with her stroller or leading Saturday morning yoga with her family. She's got healthy meal plans, protein shakes, and apps to help her stay on track. And she always finds a way to flex those muscles—who needs dumbbells when you can lift wriggly babies?

NATURAL HABITAT: *The gym*

LIKES: *Endorphins*

DISLIKES: *Standing still*

HOW TO SPOT: *Leggings, sneakers, and a smart watch make up her go-to outfit—she likes to have the option to lunge or sprint at any time!*

MONDAY

Park run

TUESDAY

Leg day

WEDNESDAY

Weight training

THURSDAY

Cardio

FRIDAY

Cycling

SATURDAY

Yoga

SUNDAY

Rest day

The last-minute mom

This mom is always in a rush. Between kids, pets, chores, and work, she has a lot to juggle, but somehow, she never drops the ball. She's likely to forget about the bake sale until the night before, but will still manage to rustle up some treats in time. Her household can be a little wild and her timekeeping might not be the best—but as long as her kids are fed and clean(ish) her job is done!

NATURAL HABITAT:
"Just around the corner!"

LIKES: The days she can find a matching pair of socks

DISLIKES: Schedules

HOW TO SPOT: Usually asking if anyone has seen her keys

NATURAL HABITAT: *In front of a spreadsheet*

LIKES: *Writing lists*

DISLIKES: *Surprises!*

HOW TO SPOT: *Always on time and never forgets to pack the PE gear*

The organized mom

This mom's organizational skills are unrivaled. The school dropoff and bedtime in her house happen like clockwork. She meticulously plans every day of every week, and manages to keep track of all birthdays, appointments, and after-school activities. If a soccer game starts at 11, she's got her family out of the door by 10:15, along with the snacks and water bottles.

The artsy mom

Knitting needles and sewing machines are this mom's idea of technology. Her family rarely needs to go shopping, because she's a pro at mending socks or knitting cozy sweaters. She believes there's no such thing as a failed project, and always finds a way to transform objects that others might throw away. She loves encouraging her kids to get creative, and she is VERY passionate about pompoms.

NATURAL HABITAT: The local craft store

LIKES: Up-cycling

DISLIKES: Buying gifts—why buy when you can make them by hand?

HOW TO SPOT: Paint-splashed clothes and an entire closet devoted to craft "essentials"

IMPRESS AN ARTSY MOM WITH AN ORIGAMI HEART

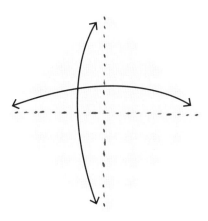

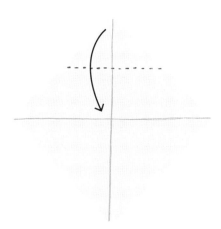

1. *Fold a square of paper in half diagonally, then open it and fold the other side to create two creases.*

2. *Open the paper out again, then fold the top corner down so the tip meets the center of the square.*

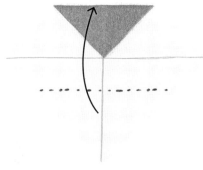

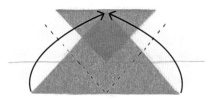

3. *Fold the bottom corner up to the very top edge.*

4. *Fold both sides in to the center.*

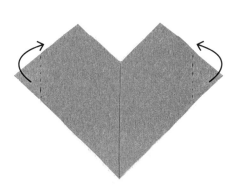

5. *Carefully fold back the two points on the sides.*

6. *Carefully fold the top two points down.*

7. *Ta-da! Your heart is ready to give.*

The rule-book mom

This mom is a stickler for the rules and always wants to get things right, especially when it comes to her family. Her bookshelf is full of books covering every stage of development from teething to teenagers. She is passionate about health and safety and can be a tad overprotective. Bike rides aren't as simple as grabbing a bike and helmet. There are fluorescent strips to be attached, bells to be tested, and bodies to be padded.

NATURAL HABITAT: In the "How to" section of a library or bookstore

LIKES: Reading the instructions

DISLIKES: Uncharted territory

HOW TO SPOT: She's the go-to guru on parenting techniques

NATURAL HABITAT: The front seat of a roller coaster

LIKES: Borrowing her kids' clothes

DISLIKES: Being predictable

HOW TO SPOT: You'll know her when you see her—she stands out from the crowd!

The rebel mom

Rebel mom encourages her kids to color outside the lines. She has a habit of zoning out when being told instructions, and prefers to find her own way. Sometimes, she's the one introducing her kids to new music, and she loves that they can enjoy lots of the same things. She sees her children as her friends, and sometimes wishes she didn't have to be the one to tell them off every now and again.

No matter the mixture of mom you know, she'll be someone who shapes who you are now, and who you'll grow up to be.

Thank you to your mom, their mom, and all the moms yet to come.

Thank you for...

Listening

Getting us dressed

Bedtime stories

Making us toast

Getting messy

Not sleeping very much

Days out

Days in

Cleaning up

Drying tears

Answering questions

Cheering us up

Hugs

Picking us up

Sharing advice

For my special and brilliant mum, Esme. x — D. A. B.
To my mom and to moms everywhere, with love. — A. L.

Brimming with creative inspiration, how-to projects, and useful information to enrich your everyday life, Quarto Knows is a favorite destination for those pursuing their interests and passions. Visit our site and dig deeper with our books into your area of interest: Quarto Creates, Quarto Cooks, Quarto Homes, Quarto Lives, Quarto Drives, Quarto Explores, Quarto Gifts, or Quarto Kids.

How to Spot a Mom © 2021 Quarto Publishing plc.
Text © 2021 Donna Amey Bhatt. Illustrations © 2021 Aura Lewis.

First published in 2021 by Wide Eyed Editions, an imprint of The Quarto Group.
100 Cummings Center, Suite 265D, Beverly, MA 01915 USA.
T +1 978-282-9590 F +1 978-283-2742 www.QuartoKnows.com

A CIP record for this book is available from the Library of Congress.

ISBN 978-0-7112-6104-4

The illustrations were created digitally
Set in Recoleta and Neutraface

Published by Georgia Amson-Bradshaw
Designed by Kate Haynes
Edited by Hannah Dove
Production by Dawn Cameron

Page 27 © Shutterstock / tofang

Manufactured in Guangdong, China CC112020

9 8 7 6 5 4 3 2 1

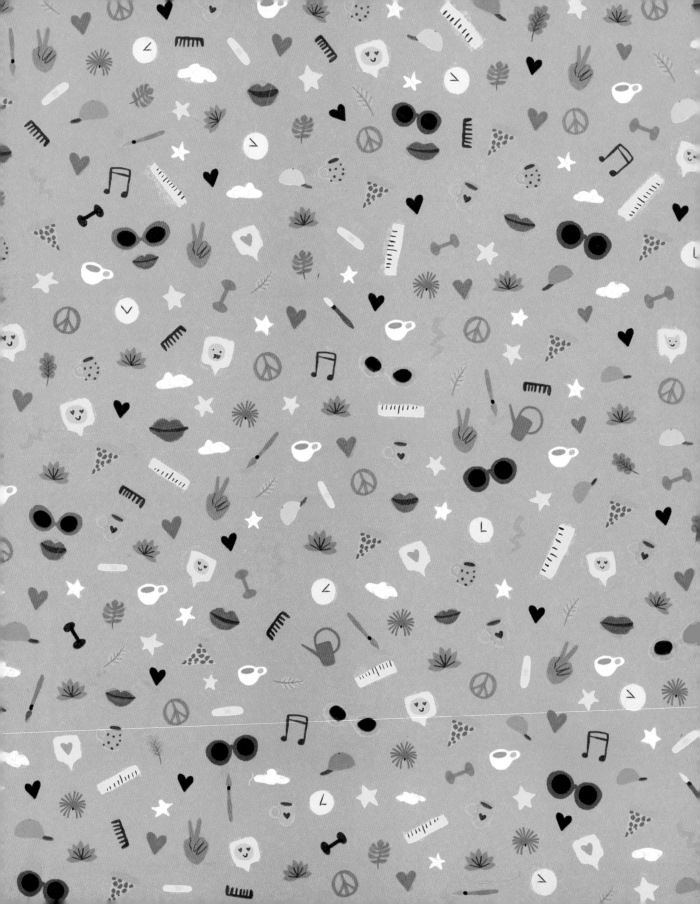